To Jeemi

in memory of our
dear little friend
"Alfie" whom we
miss very much,

Love from
Brian, Risa + Herbie

I CANNOT
LIE BY YOUR FIRE

In Loving Memory of
Man's Best Friend

Robinson Jeffers

Illustrated by Nick Bland

SOUVENIR PRESS

I've changed my ways a little; I cannot now
    now
Run with you in the evenings along the
    shore,

Except in a kind of dream; and you, if
    you dream a moment,
You see me there.

So leave awhile the paw-marks on the
    front door
Where I used to scratch to go out or in,
And you'd soon open; leave on the
    kitchen floor
The marks of my drinking-pan.

I cannot lie by your fire as I used to do
On the warm stone,

Nor at the foot of your bed; no, all the
    nights through
I lie alone.

But your kind thought has laid me less
    than six feet
Outside your window where firelight so
    often plays,

And where you sit to read — and I fear
    often grieving for me
Every night your lamplight lies on my
    place.

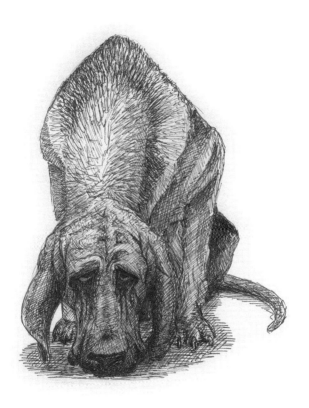

You, man and woman, live so long, it is
  hard
To think of you ever dying.
A little dog would get tired, living so
  long.

I hope that when you are lying
Under the ground like me your lives will
    appear
As good and joyful as mine.

No, dears, that's too much to hope: you
    are not so well cared for
As I have been.

And never have known the passionate
    undivided
Fidelities that I knew,

Your minds are perhaps too active, too many-sided. . . .
But to me you were true.

You were never masters, but friends. I was
    your friend.
I loved you well, and was loved. Deep
    love endures
To the end and far past the end. If this is
    my end,
I am not lonely. I am not afraid. I am still
    yours.

I Cannot Lie by Your Fire

I've changed my ways a little; I cannot now
Run with you in the evenings along the shore,
Except in a kind of dream; and you, if you dream
    a moment
You see me there.

So leave awhile the paw-marks on the front door
Where I used to scratch to go out or in,
And you'd soon open; leave on the kitchen floor
The marks of my drinking-pan.

I cannot lie by your fire as I used to do
On the warm stone,
Nor at the foot of your bed; no, all the nights
    through
I lie alone.

But your kind thought has laid me less than six feet
Outside your window where firelight so often
    plays,
And where you sit to read – and I fear often
    grieving for me
Every night your lamplight lies on my place.

You, man and woman, live so long, it is hard
To think of you ever dying.
A little dog would get tired, living so long.
I hope that when you are lying

Under the ground like me your lives will appear
As good and joyful as mine.
No, dears, that's too much hope: you are not so
    well cared for
As I have been.

And never have known the passionate undivided
Fidelities that I knew,
Your minds are perhaps too active, too many-
    sided. . . .
But to me you were true.

You were never masters, but friends. I was your
    friend.
I loved you well, and was loved. Deep love endures
To the end and far past the end. If this is my end,
I am not lonely, I am not afraid. I am still yours.

Robinson Jeffers – American poet, d.1962 aged 75.

If you need someone to talk to about your loss ...

United Kingdom
The Pet Loss Befrienders Service:
0800 0966606

This poem originally titled *The House Dog's Grave* (*Ilaig, an English bulldog*) is © 1941 by Robinson Jeffers

Copyright renewed 1969 by Donnan Jeffers and Garth Jeffers

This special gift edition first published 2001 by Souvenir Press Ltd
43 Great Russell Street, London WC1B 3PD

Reprinted 2003, 2004

© 2001 Souvenir Press Ltd and is published by arrangement with Randon House Trade Publishing, a division of Random House, Inc.

ISBN 0 285 63623 5

Printed in Singapore